STAMPS TELL THE STORY OF STAMPS

STAMPS
tell the story of
STAMPS

by Arieh Lindenbaum

 SABRA BOOKS·NEW YORK

SBN 87631–037–4
LIBRARY OF CONGRESS CATALOG CARD NUMBER 71–124117
COPYRIGHT © 1970 AMERICAN-ISRAEL PUBLISHING CO., LTD.
PRINTED IN ISRAEL BY E. LEWIN-EPSTEIN LTD., BAT YAM

By Way of Introduction . . .

Stamps, small as they are, have big stories to tell.

The little pieces of colored paper embrace history and geography, depict landscapes and seascapes and now even moonscapes, portraits of famous people, records of great achievements in literature, science, music and all the arts and also the myths and legends of peoples from all corners of the globe.

The hero of our book is The Stamp.

Whether you are a stamp collector now, become one by the time you finish this book, or prefer simply to appreciate the hobby (and skill, and sometimes obsession) of stamp collecting, we hope that you will become aware of the big world reflected in the myriad, beautiful, somber, sometimes even funny faces of stamps.

The Publishers

The Postal Stone of the Cape of Good Hope

THE CAPE OF GOOD HOPE, the southern tip of the African continent, has a very old and interesting philatelic history. It goes back before the Republic of South Africa, almost to the discovery of the Cape by Bartholomew Diaz in 1488. A short time after Diaz discovered the Cape, ships of various nations, on their way to India, stopped there to take on provisions for their voyage.

And there, on a ship bound for India, a young man who had been away from home and parents for a long time got homesick. In vain did he beg the captain to be allowed to return to his home somewhere on the shores of faraway England. Then the homesick young sailor had a brain storm. He wrote a letter to his parents and put it under a great stone on the shore of the Cape, hoping that the letter would be taken by the sailors of the next ship returning to England and delivered to his parents somehow. And sure enough (although you would scarcely believe it) the letter was taken by a sailor on his way to England and delivered to its address. This was the first attempt at finding a postal service.

The oldest postal stone, on which an engraving indicated that letters had been laid under it, bears the marks of the year 1607. With the founding of a permanent settlement at Table Bay in 1652 and the establishment of better postal service, this primitive service came to an end.

2

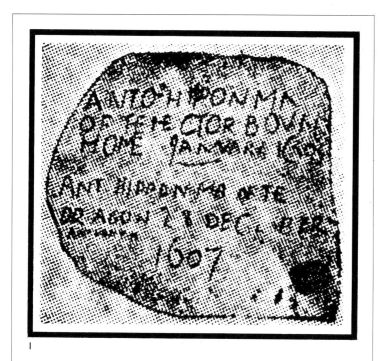

I

The First Postage Stamp in the World

S PEEDY AND SAFE transportation of the post over vast areas was a serious problem for post offices, which were established in most European countries in the nineteenth century. (News of the death of the Russian Czar Alexander III reached far-flung corners of Russia one year later.) There were no stamps and no post boxes. A letter had to be handed in at a post office and a fee paid according to the letter's destination.

In 1823 the Governor of India offered £2,000 sterling to anyone who would organize postal service that would deliver post *within 70 days* between India and Britain, and return.

Thomas Fletcher Waghorn, a British sailor, took up the challenge. He organized dispatches of mail by steamboat from Bombay in India to Suez in Egypt. From Suez to Alexandria, on the Mediterranean Sea, the mail was taken over land (the Suez Canal had not yet been built) and from there again by steamboat to England. This service began in 1839 and trimmed to 65 days the time needed for letters from England to reach India and return!

In 1835 Rowland Hill, a teacher, suggested to the British government that postage be paid by means of a stamp to be stuck on the envelope, so that postmen would not have to collect the money due for each letter. At first the idea was laughed at, but Hill persisted, and in 1840 Parliament passed the idea into law. The British public rejoiced. Now they could send letters within the country for the low price of one penny.

On May 6, 1840, the Penny Black and Two-Penny Blue stamps–the first stamps in the world–bearing the portrait of Queen Victoria, were sold throughout Britain. One interesting detail: To this day Britain does not print the name of the country on its stamps. The first British stamp did not need it, since no other countries issued stamps then. This is a privilege Britain has retained to this very day.

2

3

4

I Am the Only One Left in the World

IN 1850 SPECIAL stamps for mailing newspapers appeared in British Guiana in South America. The owners of the newspaper in Georgetown, the capital of Guiana, printed very primitive newspaper stamps—so primitive that the manager of the local post office had to initial every one of them to prevent forgeries. By 1856 the Guiana stamps were being printed in England. But that year, when they did not arrive, the Guiana Post Office manager had to ask the local newspaper, which had supplied the first stamps in 1850, to reprint them.

Very few one-cent stamps were printed, apparently; by 1873 stamp collectors had no idea of their existence. One copy of the stamp turned up by chance in the collection of a teen-age boy. Since he found no printed frame in his album for this stamp, he sold it to a neighbor for sixpence! In 1878 the neighbor's collection was bought by a British stamp dealer who sold the stamp for $750 to the foremost collector in those days, an Austrian baron living in France, Philipp Ferrari. In his will the Baron left the stamp together with his whole collection to the German Postal Museum, but the French government requisitioned it as war compensation and the stamp was sold in public auction in 1922 to an American millionaire named Hind for 300,000 francs.

An amazing story was published in an American newspaper a number of years after Hind's death. A collector found another copy of the one-cent stamp after Hind had announced the rarity of the stamp in his possession. The collector offered his stamp to Hind, and Hind agreed to pay a fantastic sum for it. After the money had been handed over and Hind had the stamp, he lit a cigar and burned it, declaring, "There is now only one one-cent Guiana stamp in the world."

5

6

The Triangles of the Cape of Good Hope

A FTER THE BRITISH conquest of the Cape of Good Hope in 1806, postal services were begun there, though stamps were not yet in use. Later, after Britain's success with penny postage and the use of gummed postage stamps, people wanted a similar postal system on the Cape, but it was not until 1853 that the first stamps appeared there. Today these stamps are the most famous in the world. They are the Cape Triangles.

About ten years earlier, it was agreed that the Cape stamps would be printed in Britain and would be completely different from those of the mother country. Negotiations for the stamps took a long time. Meanwhile the Cape government was changed and the new Governor demanded that the issue of stamps be exactly the same as the British stamps except, of course, for the country's name. The stamps were ordered in London, but because of lack of money the order was cancelled. Again years passed, and only in 1853 did the Cape stamps at long last appear—in a triangular shape and picturing what were symbols of hope among the Cape people—a beautiful woman resting on a stone, and by her side an anchor.

About eight years later, the stock of triangular stamps ran out. More stamps, ordered from England, did not arrive on time, and the Cape had to print a temporary issue in a local shop. Because of their poor and unprofessional execution, these stamps were called "wood cuts" (they are very rare). The rough stamps were used for only a short time until the missing stamps arrived.

Square stamps were introduced on the Cape in 1864, because it was simpler to print and perforate them, and the Triangles of the Cape of Good Hope were discontinued.

7

8

The Peculiar Mauritius Stamp

M AURITIUS IS AN ISLAND east of Africa. Philatelists know that the Mauritius Stamp is one of the rarest in the world. Here is the reason. One day in 1847 the wife of the island's Governor decided she wanted to send invitations to a party by mail. There were no postage stamps for the island yet, so she persuaded her husband to print some.

She showed the owner of a small printing press (actually, he dealt more in repairing clocks than in printing) one of the first British stamps to use as a model. At the top of the stamp the Governor's wife wanted the word "Postage," at the bottom the value of one penny, along the right side the name "Mauritius," and along the left the words "Post Paid."

The clockmaker certainly had no idea that because of his bad memory the stamp he printed was to become one of the rarest and most expensive in history.

While he was cutting the block the clockmaker forgot the words "Post Paid" and instead engraved "Post Office." Stamps with the correct inscription appeared only eight months later, because at first nobody noticed the mistake. Today the faulty Mauritius stamps are available only in rare single copies, and their catalogue price is thousands of dollars. Two of them are to be found in the stamp collection of the British Royal Family.

9

10

King "Bomba"

FERDINAND I WAS a tyrant king. His kingdom included southern Italy, with Naples as its capital, and the island of Sicily, and his rule there, in the early 1800's, was marked by arrests and murders. This tradition was carried on by his grandson, Ferdinand II, who was given the nickname "Bomba" because he was a braggart and a tyrant.

Seeing the success of Rowland Hill's postal reforms in England, Ferdinand II ordered a similar reform and issued stamps in his kingdom. In that 1859 series were seven values showing the head of the king. At first Ferdinand refused to allow his portrait to appear on the stamps, because he did not want his likeness sullied by postmarks! So a special postmark in the form of a wreathed garland was made, empty in the middle so that it would mark only the edges of the stamps, thus cancelling them but not obliterating the head of the tyrant.

11

12

The Oldest Man in the World

IN THE FIFTIES a competition took place between the Soviet Union and Colombia on a very peculiar subject: Which of these two countries had the oldest man alive? It is peculiar, too, that this competition came about because of postage stamps.

In 1957 the Soviet Post Office issued a stamp bearing the portrait of Machmud Evasov, who was living on a state farm in the Soviet Union and who was thought to be the oldest man alive. When the stamp was issued Evasov was 148 years old.

While the Russian was enjoying world fame and serving as publicity for the good life in the Soviet Union, a citizen of Colombia came forward–Javier Pereira, who was born on December 28, 1787, and was 169 years old! The Colombian Post Office, wishing to outdo the Russian stamp of Evasov, issued a stamp showing the head of Javier Pereira, with the explanation for his longevity: "Don't take anything to heart, smoke the best cigarettes, and drink the finest Colombian coffee"!

Now, it is hard to determine the age of the oldest men, but there is no doubt that these two men were much older than 120. The Colombian was invited to the United States in 1957. Doctors examined him and determined that he was more than 150 years old. Pereira died in 1958, and according to the Colombian version, he was 171 years old. Evasov, the Russian, died in 1959 at the age of 149.

13

14

The Dove of Basel

IN 1845 THE SWISS POST OFFICE issued a stamp showing a dove holding a leaf in its mouth. It is not especially expensive, though it is most rare in blocks of two or more. For many years very few people knew the Basel "dove stamps" existed. It became known only a few years ago that a set was in existence, and this is how it happened.

One day a Swiss sent his old writing desk, inherited from his ancestors, to a carpenter to be repaired. To his great surprise, in a corner of the desk the carpenter found part of a sheet of stamps—the now famous "dove stamps." They had been bought by a former owner of the desk, had gotten lost in a corner, and had been preserved for decades as if they had only just been bought at the post office.

The owner of the desk was not particularly interested in the stamps, in spite of their rarity; the thousands of dollars he sold them for were of far greater interest to him. Today the stamps, bought by a Swiss shoe manufacturer and donated to the Postal Museum of Switzerland, are seen by thousands of visitors.

15

Biafra's Rise and Fall

JUST BECAUSE stamps depict the history of the world, its peoples and its states, they also reflect the grandeurs and the tragedies of history.

Look, for instance, at these stamps issued by the short-lived, independent African Republic of Biafra.

The Ibo tribe, living in the eastern region of Nigeria, declared their independence on May 30, 1967.

Their postage stamps symbolized their independence. Their first stamps appeared in February 1968, were printed in Lisbon, the capital of Portugal, and were for three values: the two-penny shows a map of independent Biafra; the second stamp shows the emblem of the State against the historic date of May 30, 1967; the third stamp shows a mother carrying a baby in her arms. This first series was bright and optimistic.

Then came the devastating war in which Biafra defended itself against Nigeria, with primitive weapons and in starvation conditions, and with tragic consequences for its people.

The second series, issued later in 1968, comprising five stamps, bears witness to the plight of Biafra.

One stamp shows a memorial monument to 30,000 of the Ibo tribe who were slaughtered in one cruel massacre in 1966; two other stamps show a camp with refugees being treated by nurses of the Ibo tribe.

During 1969, conditions deteriorated alarmingly, supply lines were cut off, and millions faced starvation and death. Biafra fell early in 1970.

Its stamps tell the story of its rise and fall.

16

17

18

The Stamp That Built the Panama Canal

WERE YOU AWARE that the famous Panama Canal was built in Panama thanks to a small, ordinary stamp? This is the story.

The Canal was begun in 1881 in Panama by French engineers, but extraordinary difficulties, complicated by epidemics, halted the work. The American public then favored a proposal made by Nicaragua to build a canal through its territory, and the American Senate was ready to budget the money for a Nicaraguan canal.

Bonnet Verela, one of the French engineers, was unhappy with the new plan, but he couldn't re-interest the Congress in the idea of a Panamanian canal. One day, the despondent Verela, walking along the sidewalk in Washington, D. C., saw newspaper headlines telling of a disaster in Nicaragua—a volcano had erupted, killing thousands of people, and it had happened in the area where the Nicaraguan canal was to be built!

Bonnet Verela's hopes for a Panamanian canal were revived. But then the president of Nicaragua, who had a financial interest in getting the canal for his country, announced that the "rumors" of volcanic eruptions in Nicaragua were untrue. Verela had to fight back fast, before the Congress voted funds to the Nicaraguan project.

As luck would have it, just then Verela got a letter from a friend, and on the envelope was a Nicaraguan stamp that made Verela jump for joy. The ordinary two-cent stamp was worth a great deal to Verela, for it pictured active volcanoes in Nicaragua!

Verela bought hundreds of these stamps and sent them to every American congressman. The stamps achieved their purpose. Congress ratified the plan for the Panama Canal.

19

Each Man Has His Own Caricature

CARICATURES ARE drawings that show a person in an exaggerated and distorted form in order to make an amusing impression. You wouldn't expect sedate and dignified postal ministers to issue funny stamps, but that's just what they did in Czechoslovakia in 1968.

The stamps caricature seven famous men of the twentieth century. One of them is the great film comic Charlie Chaplin, whose funny face made millions laugh in the 1920's.

A second series of caricatures that appeared in Czechoslovakia in 1969: Hviezdoslav (1849–1921) a Slovakian poet; G.K. Chesterton (1874–1936) a famous English literary critic, known to readers as a writer of detective stories and the inventor of "Father Brown"; Vladimir Mayakovsky (1893–1930) a great modern Russian playwright and poet; Henri Matisse (1869–1954) a famous French impressionist painter; Ales Hrdlicka (1896–1943) a Czech-born American anthropologist. The last stamp in this series was dedicated to the world-famous Czech writer and playwright, Franz Kafka (1883–1924) who wrote his works in German.

20

21   22   23

Goya's Immoral Painting

POSTAGE STAMPS BASED on famous paintings have appeared in many countries. The works of the famous Spanish painter Francisco Goya have been put on stamps a number of times. In 1930, on the centenary of the painter's death, Spain issued a series of commemorative stamps, one of them showing Goya's well-known painting "Naked Maja." The stamp with the nude portrait was displayed in an exhibition that year in Seville, Spain, and it aroused a furor that led finally to the resignation of the government.

At the height of the storm a new government was formed in Spain. It remained quiet on the question of the painting's artistic value, and in spite of protests from all over the world, the stamp remained in circulation.

Goya didn't agree that the painting was immoral. In his opinion, dress by itself was no indication of morality. He painted another, sarcastic picture of Maja–"Maja Clothed." As for Maja, she has appeared on a number of postage stamps both naked and clothed.

24

24

25

Do Not Covet Thy Neighbor's Stamp

THE FIRST HAWAIIAN stamps were called "the Hawaiian Missionaries," because most of the mail from Hawaii then, about 1850, was that of missionaries. Today there are only a few copies of the Missionaries left. One of them was mixed up in an affair that made newspaper headlines.

One day in June 1892 the Paris police got a telephone call from the rich merchant Gaston Larrue's chambermaid. Monsieur Larrue was not opening his study door, and the maid was worried. When the police arrived, they found Larrue had been murdered. All money and gold coins in his room had been left as they were, so the police assumed that the murderer had been interrupted and that he had fled.

Then one of the police noticed that Larrue had been a stamp collector, and when he compared the contents of Larrue's album with Larrue's list of stamps, he saw that one of the stamps was missing from the album. The marks were still clear where the Hawaiian two-cent stamp of 1850 had been.

Upon questioning, a stamp dealer named Hector Goirot told the police that Gaston Larrue would not sell that stamp no matter how much Goirot had offered Larrue for it. One of the secret police investigators made friends with Goirot. Gradually he became acquainted with Goirot's collection, and in one of the dealer's albums he discovered, to his amazement, a complete set of the Hawaiian stamps of 1850. He noticed that the two-cent stamp looked as if it had just been added.

Hector Goirot was arrested, and later he confessed that he had murdered for the tiny piece of paper that was the two-cent Hawaiian stamp.

26

Millie the Swearing Parrot

M ILLIE IS AN ENGLISH- and French-speaking parrot. She was to be one of the main attractions in the Guyana Pavilion at Expo '67, an international exhibition held in Montreal. The participating countries sent their best exhibits, especially in the field of entertainment. Guyana sent Millie the Parrot, who had learned greetings in English and in French.

Now, at the opening ceremony of the show, Millie forgot all her good manners and began uttering curses that only a sergeant major could possibly compete with, according to newspaper stories of the incident. The officials of the exhibition banished Millie, and the parrot was transferred to the zoo.

The Guyana Post Office swallowed this bitter pill but decided to honor the parrot, and at Christmas that year it issued two commemorative stamps on which Millie is depicted in all her glory.

CHRISTMAS
1967

'MILLIE'
THE BILINGUAL PARROT
EXPO 67

25 CENTS

GUYANA
SOUTH AMERICA

27

Better Safe Than Sorry

THERE ARE ABOUT 50,000 people living in the New Hebrides Islands in the South Pacific, and most of them are farmers. Many of their customs are based on folktales that have been passed down from generation to generation. Three stamps issued in 1969 were based on one of these legends.

There was once a woman of the islands, a shrew if ever there was one. Even worse, she did not listen to her husband. When he decided to teach her a lesson, she ran away from home, her husband in full pursuit. During the chase they found themselves at the top of a tall tree. The wife challenged her husband to prove his courage by jumping from the tree. He agreed to do it if his wife would jump from the tree too. The woman deceived her husband by tying a climbing vine to her heel. When the two of them jumped from the tree, the husband was killed while the wife was left hanging by the vine and so was saved from death.

The pride of the New Hebrides men was badly wounded. Since that time, for many generations, the men have jumped from a tall tower to prove their courage. Once a year all the people gather for a festival, and the main event is the men's jump from wooden towers especially built for this purpose. Nowadays the men tie a climbing vine to their legs just as the clever woman did, for after all, it is better to be safe than sorry.

28

29

30

31

The Battle for Iwo Jima

BATTLES AND WARS have often been recorded on postage stamps. One interesting stamp of the United States is commemorative of the battle of Iwo Jima in the Second World War.

The island of Iwo Jima had become a Japanese fortress and its airfield was a hindrance to the Americans in their operations against Japan. Eight companies of Marines landed on the island in February 1945 and succeeded in cutting the Japanese chain of defense. The Americans suffered heavy losses in the battle for the island, which went on for two months. They had to fight for every inch of the way. When the Americans reached the top of Mount Suribachi, five soldiers went to the summit and raised the American flag. This dramatic moment was photographed by one of the Marines. When the picture reached the United States, a monument in memory of the brave Marines was put up and a commemorative stamp issued, based on the same photograph. The monument stands in Washington and the stamp adds one more moment of history to stamp collections over the world.

31

Postal Service on the Moon

THE HISTORIC MOON landing in 1969 was recorded in a postage stamp and a unique postmark: the moon. The three Apollo 11 astronauts took with them a special postmark reading, "Moon landing July 20, 1969, U.S.A." Besides putting this historic event on record with a commemorative postmark, they also wanted to test the lunar influence on ink taken into space. Now there is one envelope actually postmarked in space. It is on exhibit in the National Museum of the Smithsonian Institution in Washington.

The original block used in space was returned to earth and given special disinfectant treatment before it was flown to Washington for printing the 120 million stamps commemorating the moon flight.

32

33

The Murderer Stamp

ONE DAY IN MAY 1926 a middle-aged man was strolling in Avenue St. Michele, in Paris, holding a small photograph in his hand. He kept looking at the photograph and at the passers-by as though he was looking for someone. Suddenly he grew excited, looked at the picture, went up to one of the passers-by and asked, "Are you Petlyura?" When the other answered that he was, the man drew out a revolver, fired at Petlyura and killed him.

The killer was Shalom Shvartzbard; the murdered man was Symon Petlyura, who had ruled in the Ukraine for a time.

Shalom Shvartzbard, a soldier and Russian poet, served in the French army in the First World War and afterwards volunteered for the French Legion and was sent to the Ukraine to help the White Russians fight the communists. There he witnessed deeds of cruelty and slaughter by Petlyura's men against the Jews.

In 1919, Shvartzbard went to Paris and took up his old occupation, clockmaking. One day he read in the newspaper that Petlyura was living in Paris. The thought that the man responsible for the murder of so many of his fellow Jews was living comfortably in Paris gave him no rest. Shvartzbard had never seen Petlyura, but in an encyclopedia he found Petlyura's portrait on a stamp, and that was the picture he took with him in the hope of meeting the murderer on the street.

Luck was with him. He met Petlyura and took revenge, then stood serenely by until the police arrived. Shvartzbard's trial was an historic one. At that time the term genocide was not used, and the principles governing the Nuremberg Trials had not been established. Shvartzbard undertook his own defense, and in 1927 the jury acquitted him. In this tragedy, a tiny postage stamp played a great part.

34

Ships Trapped in the Suez Canal

THE LOCAL POSTAL services organized on the fourteen merchant ships trapped in the Suez Canal since 1967 are an interesting episode in philately. The ships, belonging to a number of countries, have been there since the Six Day War in June 1967, trapped between Israel and Egypt in the Great Bitter Lake in the Suez Canal area.

A few months after the war the crews of the ships set up an association called the Great Bitter Lake Association. One of its projects was a local postal service with special stamps. One of the ships' commanders, an enthusiastic philatelist, drew up a unique series of stamps. The stamps were "printed" on a primitive duplicating machine aboard one of the ships, colored by hand with ink or paint, and then distributed among the fourteen crews.

The stamps are really just labels, meant to direct public attention to the trapped boats and men. They are not recognized by the Universal Postal Union (U.P.U.). The labels are stuck on letters going out from the boats and are franked with special postmarks of each boat, but in Port Tawfiq on the Egyptian side of the Canal official Egyptian stamps are stuck on by the U.P.U. and then the letters with both stamps go out to all corners of the earth.

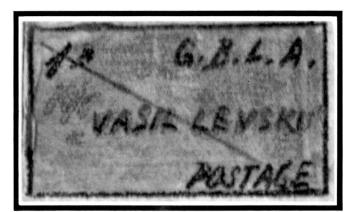

35

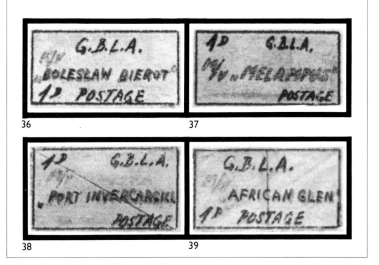

36

37

38

39

A State with Only Three Post Offices

ON THE SLOPES of the Himalaya Mountains lies a small independent state which, though it is not a member of the Universal Postal Union, does issue stamps and runs a postal service. This state is Bhutan.

Bhutan opened its first post office in Tinpu, one of the two capitals of the state, in the sixties. Before it opened, mail used to be carried by runners between the many mountain strongholds of Bhutan. Today there are about 300,000 people and three post offices in that little state.

Though the Bhutanese mail service does not require postage stamps at all, the government has issued stamps since 1966 and sold them abroad to bring in money. The stamps' illustrations are dedicated to the "Abominable Snowman" about whom everyone in the Himalayas talks but no one has ever seen.

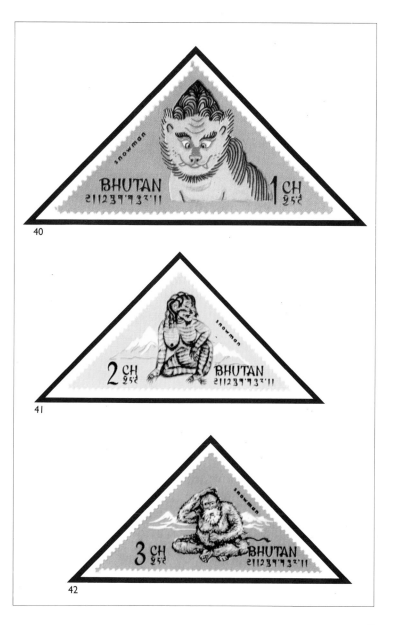

40

41

42

Two Stamps—One Man

ONLY ONCE HAVE two countries issued identical stamps–the same shape, the same face value, and the same picture. In 1969 both West Germany, the birthplace of Alexander von Humboldt, and Venezuela issued a stamp honoring the two-hundredth anniversary of the death of von Humboldt. Von Humboldt, a natural scientist and a great scholar, is considered the father of physical geography. A range of mountains, a river, a marshland, and a mountain in Peru are named after him.

It has happened that stamps have been issued from the same drawing by the same artist in different countries, but each country changes its stamp in some detail, in form, in color, or at least in value. But in the case of the von Humboldt stamps, the Venezuelan and the West German stamps were absolutely identical, except of course for the name of the country.

43

44

The Triumph of Weak King Soundita

IN AFRICA, FOLKSONGS and legends have been passed from mouth to mouth and from generation to generation. Six of the best-known legends of West Africa have found a place on the postage stamps of Guinea.

Each stamp has its own story. The last stamp in the series, the 200-franc stamp, recalls the death of King Soumangourou at the hands of the maiden Djegue. The legend goes back to the thirteenth century, a time of conflict among many kings. The strongest of them all was Soumangourou.

Soundita, the son of King Famangan, was a weak man but a strong enemy of Soumangourou. When Soundita succeeded to his father's throne he vowed that he would also rule over Soumangourou's kingdom. He offered his sister Djegue to be Soumangourou's wife, for he knew he could conquer Soumangourou only through cunning. Djegue quickly discovered the secret of Soumangourou's life—that he could be killed only by a black and white arrow. Mounting her white horse, Djegue galloped to her brother, King Soundita, and told him the secret. That is how Soundita the feeble defeated Soumangourou the strong and fulfilled his vow.

SOUMANGOUROU KANTE TUE PAR DJEGUE

REPUBLIQUE DE GUINEE 200 F

45

LEUR LE LIEVRE VEND LA SOEUR

REPUBLIQUE DE GUINEE 75 F

46

L'HERITAGE DU VIEUX FAYA

REPUBLIQUE DE GUINEE 100 F

47

What's the Difference Between Schubert and Schumann?

THE WORSE THE ERRORS on postage stamps, the better philatelists like it. An interesting case is that of stamps portraying the composer Schumann. The East German Post Office issued two commemorative stamps in 1956 on the hundredth anniversary of the death of the great composer Robert Alexander Schumann. The plan was to print Schumann's portrait on a background of his music, but by mistake the portrait of Schumann was printed against a background of notes composed by Franz Schubert.

The error was soon discovered, and the East German Post Office stopped selling the stamps. Two others were printed in the same colors and of the same face values—and this time Schumann appears on the background of his own notes. In the illustrations here you can easily see the difference even if you cannot read music. The stamp with the error has three musical phrases in the lefthand corner, while the correct stamp has only one.

This affair deeply embarrassed the heads of the East German Post Office, but the collectors who had gotten the stamps before they were removed from sale were very happy.

48

49

Great Men-Great Hobbies

W HO HAS NOT heard of Winston Churchill, the great British
statesman, who led Britain to victory over Nazi Germany
in the Second World War? And who has not heard of Churchill's
contemporary, the President of the United States of America,
Franklin Delano Roosevelt? But does everybody know that
Winston Churchill was a talented painter and Franklin Roosevelt
was an enthusiastic stamp collector?

Churchill's paintings were printed in the form of stamps issued
by Grenada, the spice island in the Caribbean Sea.

Churchill always said, wrote and persuaded people that every
person needs a hobby because in his opinion, a hobby enriches a
man's life and enables him to live longer. His favorite hobby was
painting.

President Roosevelt also believed in hobbies. He was a great
stamp collector.

In recent years "Churchill Stamps" have been sold for more
than half a million dollars.

50

51

52

Right or Left?

S OMETIMES COUNTRIES are not too careful about the details of their stamps. The East German stamp dedicated to the memory of Schumann and which appeared with Schubert's music is not the only example. In East Germany a stamp was issued showing the German author Thomas Mann wearing the parting in his hair on the right side. However, if you look at the stamp published in honor of Mann by West Germany, you will see immediately that the late author wore the parting in his hair on the left side.

53

54

Stamps Drawn By Children

IN RECENT YEARS a number of countries have issued stamps of children's drawings. Britain issued two Christmas stamps in 1966 showing the work of six-year-old children. They were the winners of a competition held among hundreds of children, and for their work each won a prize of £20. The Christmas stamps show one of the three kings famous in Christian tradition, and a snowman. A drawing was also chosen for the Christmas "First Day" cover, and its young creator won a prize of £10.

55

56

57

Stamps That Never Appeared

IN 1946, AUSTRIA, which had fought on the side of Hitler's Germany in the Second World War, proclaimed to the world, "We shall never forget." The slogan was used on a series of stamps Austria printed to express its sorrow for the tragic events that followed. The stamps depicted the Nazi horrors. Two stamps, the first sheets already printed, were not approved by the Occupation Powers of the Allies in Austria. One stamp showed a map of Austria with the dates 1935–1945, swastikas, and strokes of lightning in the form of the letters *S.S.* The other stamp showed Hitler's face as a death skull, revealing his true character.

The Allies rejected the stamps because they feared that, in the course of time, the significance of the drawings would be forgotten, and only Hitler's face would fill the albums of young people. However, now Austria is exhibiting these stamps at philatelic exhibitions.

58

59

Stamps in the Service of War

A<small>T THE BOTTOM</small> of Lake Toepliz in Austria, treasure was found in 1959–chests full of money and stamps. Because they were in sealed cases, they had not been damaged at all in spite of their long rest underwater.

The stamps were forgeries the Nazis had prepared for distribution in England, to create confusion and suspicion.

Some of the forgeries actually had been distributed during the war. The Nazi stamps looked like the English stamps bearing the portrait of King George V. But instead of the cross on the British crown, the Nazis put the Shield of David, the Jewish emblem. On forgeries of an English stamp that had appeared in 1935, the cross had been replaced by the Shield of David; the British state emblem on the righthand side was replaced by the hammer and sickle, the Soviet emblem; instead of the words "Silver Jubilee," there now was "This War Is a Jewish War" (spelled wrongly by the Nazis!); instead of the head of King George, the head of Stalin, the leader of the Soviet Union at that time.

The Allies counterattacked. They forged changes on original German stamps, one of which carried the head of Hitler. On this stamp Hitler's face was replaced by a skull. Instead of the words *Deutsches Reich* (the German Republic), they wrote *Putsches Reich* (the Lost Republic).

In the concentration camp Sachsenhausen, the Nazis forced skilled Jewish printers to make millions of forged bills and stamps. With the approach of the American army, the Nazis gave orders to burn all the forged materials. A stock of cash and stamps that had not been burned was sealed in cases and thrown into the little lake of Toepliz, in Austria, where it was found by accident fourteen years later.

60

61

62

63

64

The Greatest Collector of All

THE GREATEST collector of all time was the German baron Philipp Ferrari. An invalid, Ferrari began collecting stamps when he was very young. When he inherited a huge fortune, he dedicated it entirely to philately. He roamed the world looking for rare stamps. In Ferrari's collection not a thing was missing— not even the one-cent British Guiana stamp, the only one in the world, which he bought at a public auction. There was no stamp nor any collection for which Ferrari was not prepared to pay any price asked.

When Ferrari died in 1917, his fabulous collection was willed to the German Postal Museum, but in the First World War the collection was requisitioned by the French government and sold by the Occupation Powers to pay compensation.

Maurice Boros is considered to be Philipp Ferrari's heir in the stamp business. He is a rich tobacco merchant who bought a part of Ferrari's estate. Though Boros invested vast sums of money in acquiring expensive stamps, he never achieved the status of the "king of the philatelists," Philipp Ferrari.

The stamp-crazy baron Ferrari appeared on a special postage stamp in the princedom of Lichtenstein in 1968. Two other stamps were issued for other men who became world-famous in philately. The second stamp in this series shows Rowland Hill of Britain, who introduced the idea of a postage stamp, and the third is dedicated to Maurice Boros, the philatelic heir of Philipp Ferrari.

SIR ROWLAND HILL

FURSTENTUM LIECHTENSTEIN

1795 20 1879

65

MAURICE BURRUS

FURSTENTUM LIECHTENSTEIN

1882 1 Fr 1959

66

PHILIPPE DE FERRARI

FURSTENTUM LIECHTENSTEIN

1848 30 1917

67

59

Elijah the Prophet in a Top Hat

I N THE SECOND BOOK of Kings, chapter two, verse eleven, we read: "And it came to pass, as they still went on, and talked, that, behold, there appeared a chariot of fire, and horses of fire, which parted them both asunder; and Elijah went up by a whirlwind into heaven." This passage from the Bible has become the subject of many legends and works of art by great poets and painters. It has also found its way onto stamps—two stamps from the Vatican and one from Sweden. The pictures on them have a chariot and horseman going up in a whirlwind to heaven, but the prophet, as he is depicted on the Swedish stamp, reminds one more of a gentleman of the nineteenth century than of a prophet of the period of the First Temple.

The Swedish stamp was issued to honor the poet Eric Axel Cartfeldt, who wrote the famous poem, "The Ascension of Elijah to Heaven." This poem inspired an artist to paint a picture of the ascension. This was the picture used on the stamp. The painting, and thus the Swedish stamp, is somewhat strange. While on the Vatican stamp Elijah is seen against a background of flames and horses of fire, the Swedish Elijah is portrayed as an adorned priest dressed in a top hat and riding in a stylish carriage harnessed to a pair of white horses.

68

69

Israel's First Stamps

ON MAY 14, 1948, the State of Israel was established and the first Israeli stamps were issued. They do not carry the name Israel because down to the very last moment there was great confusion about exactly what name the state would carry. Even after the United Nations had resolved to establish the State of Israel, no final decision was made about the new state's name.

Preparations for printing the first Israeli stamps were done in the utmost secrecy. At the last moment, four artists were given 24 hours to submit sketches for the stamps.

Preparations for the stamps were done underground, for those were the days of the struggle for the establishment of the state both in the political sphere and on the battlefield, with the Arabs pressing the Jews hard. As the men worked, the whistle of bullets could be heard on the outskirts of Tel Aviv.

The time was getting short, and still the men responsible for planning the stamps did not know what name to put on them. "Judea" was then a popular name; another was "The Land of Israel," which was the name of the country before statehood; a third was simply "Israel."

The first Minister of Posts of Israel, David Remez, decided on "Judea," but at the last moment he changed his mind in favor of *Doar Ivri*, the Hebrew phrase for "Hebrew Post." The stamps with the word "Judea" were shelved and the printing of the *Doar Ivri* stamps was hurriedly begun. The printers worked day and night without let-up so that, on May 14, the new stamps were ready for the new state.

70

71

72

Index to Stamps